Discovery CHANNEL

WICKED WEATHER

WHEN EVERYTHING GOES RIGHT, IT GOES SO WRONG

Written by Mark Shulman
Contributing consultant: Jeriann Ritter, certified meteorologist

Meredith® Books
Des Moines, Iowa

Jane Root, Executive Vice President & General Manager, Discovery Channel
Carol LeBlanc, Vice President, Licensing
Elizabeth Bakacs, Vice President, Creative Services
Maren Herzog, Manager, Creative Services
Caitlin Erb, Marketing Associate

www.discovery.com

First Edition.

Printed in China.

ISBN 978-0-696-23689-1 (perfect bound)
ISBN 978-0-696-23277-0 (saddle stitch)

We welcome your comments and suggestions.
Write to us at: Meredith Books, 1716 Locust Street,
Des Moines, Iowa 50309-3023
Visit us at meredithbooks.com

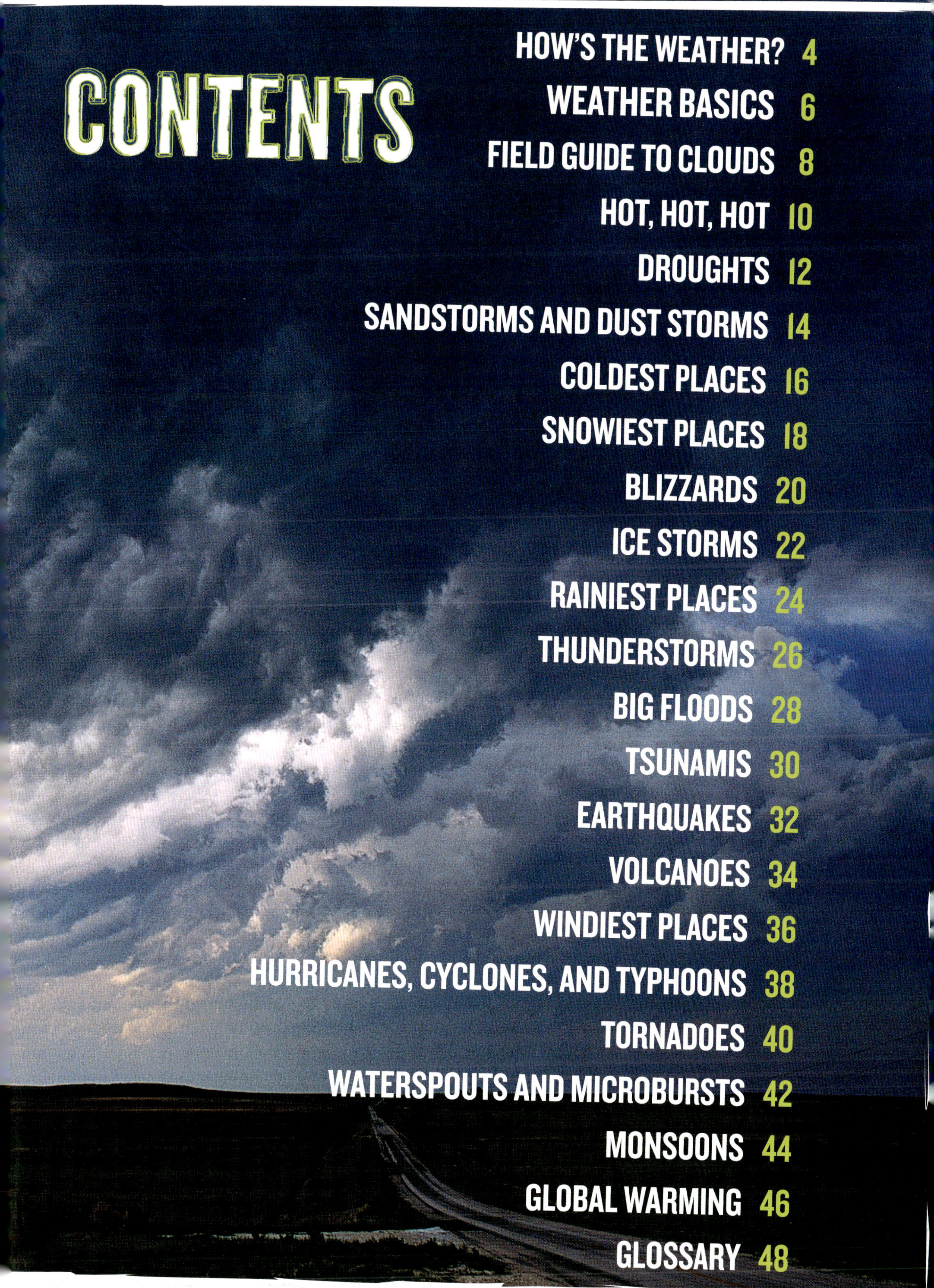

CONTENTS

HOW'S THE WEATHE

IT'S HOT! IT'S COOL! IT'S WILD! IT'S OUT OF CONTROL!

Whether or not you pay attention, the weather affects every part of your life. Don't believe it? What are your plans for today? Can you do them in a tornado? In three feet of snow? In a flood? In a heat wave? Probably not.

What is weather? It's what's happening in the atmosphere any place any time. Weather can change at any moment, depending on which way the wind blows (and how fast). In addition to atmospheric conditions, weather is affected by the sun, bodies of water, the Earth's movement, and even volcanoes and earthquakes. Weather influences your health, your wealth, the farms that produce the food you eat, and where you'll sleep tonight. Weather kills and weather brings new life.

• • •

There's a lot of weather raging inside *Wicked Weather*. This book features the best resources from Discovery Channel to give you an inside view of hurricanes, to clear the air about fog, and to be enlightening about lightning (without being frightening).

Put down your umbrella—it's raining cool facts. Soak 'em in.

WEATHER

Earth's weather doesn't take place in outer space. It happens in the layer of the atmosphere that's closest to the surface of the Earth. This part of the atmosphere is called the troposphere, otherwise known as the sky. It's where the air is.

The weather can be extremely different around the world at different times of year. But only three conditions in the atmosphere affect the weather and determine what you wear when you go out—if you go out at all. Slight variations in any of these conditions can cause a major shift in the weather. They are:

TEMPERATURE Temperature is the measure of hot or cold in degrees of Fahrenheit or Celsius. The sun and the seasons have a profound effect on how warm or cold the weather will be. But you knew that already, so we'll move on...

AIR PRESSURE Air pressure is the weight and pressure that the air high above Earth exerts on the lower air, down where you live. Why doesn't all that pressure squish you? Because your body is filled with air that acts as an opposing force. What's the effect on the planet? There are two pressure systems locked in a continuous battle to control the weather.

High Pressure Areas: You might expect storms from something called a high pressure system, but it usually brings nice weather. The higher pressure pushes the warmer air down. Clouds don't gather because the air isn't rising, it's sinking.

Low Pressure Areas: The pressure from above is low, so the air rises in the atmosphere, bringing the cold air higher. Up goes the moisture. And here come the clouds, the storms, and the precipitation.

WEATHER FRONTS When the temperature or the air pressure changes, there's a name for the borderline between the new weather and the old. It's called a weather front. Whenever a front approaches, you know the weather won't stay the same for long. Fronts lift the air up and cool or warm it to produce clouds and precipitation. The type of pressure surrounding the front determines the weather we end up with.

Watch the forecast on TV tonight to see what is predicted to happen tomorrow.

BASICS

MEASURE FOR MEASURE

The devices used to measure the weather:

Temperature: Thermometers
Mercury rises with heat; measured in degrees

Rainfall: Rain gauges
Water collected in cups; measured in inches

Snowfall: Snow boards
Snow falls on a long board; measured in inches

Wind speed: Anemometers
Wind turns a sideways windmill; measured in miles per hour or knots

kt

hPa

Air pressure: Barometers
As air pressure builds, gauge rises; measured in hectopascals

FIELD GUIDE TO

What do you see when you look at the clouds? Whales? Bunnies? There are more to clouds than just interesting shapes and animals. There are clues in the clouds that indicate what the weather is like and what is likely to happen in the next 6 to 24 hours. Ancient sailors and modern jet pilots have used knowledge of the clouds to predict the weather, and so can you.

Stratocumulus

Cumulus

LOW CLOUDS (up to 6,500 feet)

Stratus

If You See: gray clouds that cover the whole sky like a fog

Expect: a dreary, gray day; light mist or drizzle

Stratocumulus

If You See: low, lumpy gray cloud layers with clear sky in between

Expect: weak, low-intensity rain or snow

Nimbostratus

If You See: thick, continuous layers of dark gray clouds, with a ragged base

Expect: light or moderate rain or snow

MIDDLE CLOUDS (6,500 to 18,000 feet)

Altostratus

If You See: gray or blue-gray clouds covering the entire sky

Expect: coming storms that will produce continuous rain or snow in 6 to 12 hours

Altocumulus

If You See: gray, puffy masses in sometimes-parallel groups

Expect: on a warm, humid summer morning, upcoming thunderstorms in 6 to 12 hours

CLOUDS

HIGH CLOUDS (above 18,000 feet)

Cirrus

If You See: thin, wispy clouds moving across the sky from west to east

Expect: fair to pleasant weather

Cirrostratus

If You See: thin, transparent, sheetlike clouds covering the entire sky

Expect: rain or snowstorm in 12 to 24 hours

Cirrocumulus

If You See: small, rounded, white puffs with ripples (like fish scales)

Expect: fair but cold weather in winter; in the tropics, a possible hurricane

CLOUDS WITH VERTICAL DEVELOPMENT

Cumulus

If You See: fluffy balls of cotton with a flat base

Expect: any weather! (Cumulus clouds mainly form in the daytime and have a life span of 5 to 40 minutes.)

Cumulonimbus

If You See: towering clouds growing up with a dark base; tops flattened by high winds

Expect: heavy rain, hail, thunderstorms, and lightning

HOT, HOT,

If you think 105°F is a high temperature, you're not even warm. There are places on Earth where you can fry an egg on a sidewalk (if you can find a sidewalk) every day of the year. And then add humidity—the water vapor in the air. When there's a lot and the water vapor heats up, the "apparent temperature" can feel another 15 to 20 degrees warmer.

RED HOT AND BLUE In the United States, there are plenty of hot places. Arizona, Nevada, and California have the nation's hottest places with Arizona averaging July temperatures of 111°F. On July 10, 1913, California's Death Valley, which usually averages 115°F in July, registered the Western Hemisphere's highest official temperature: 134°F. Key West is the hottest place year round in the United States when you average all 12 months at 78.1°F. Phoenix and Las Vegas are the hottest large cities in America.

JUST DESERTS

Not surprisingly, the planet's most sizzling scenery is in its deserts. Temperatures in Algeria, which stretches into Africa's Sahara Desert, average higher than 90°F and regularly reach 116°F in July. Nearby Mali is nearly as hot. When it comes to large cities, the heat is really on in Bangkok, Thailand. Daily temperatures there almost always reach 90°F—and the high humidity makes it feel more like 120°F. For the world's highest verified temperature, look to North Africa's El Azizia in Libya. On September 13, 1922, it was a roasting 136°F.

HOT

HOT CHILE

For dry, dry days, you can't beat the Atacama Desert in Chile. Dozens of years can go by without rain, snow, sleet, or hail. For dry days in the United States, you have to go back to Death Valley. If you want to, that is.

DROUGHTS

Droughts don't have the force of a thunderstorm, the impact of a tornado, or the assault of a volcano. But in just 40 years, droughts worldwide have caused millions of deaths. And the economy suffers too. Droughts are the most costly natural disasters in America. Usually droughts cost the United States about $8 billion per year.

When does a dry spell qualify as a drought? If a month or more has gone by with less than 30 percent of the usual precipitation, it's a drought. Some last for months, others for years.

In the United States, droughts can occur anywhere. You tend to hear about the droughts in the Midwest because most farms in that region don't use irrigation. Any slowdown in rainfall there will immediately affect residents, crops, and food prices for months to come.

DROUGHT EFFECTS

Droughts affect more than just farmers—they can affect you! When the demand for water is bigger than the supply, you begin to feel the effects of a socioeconomic drought. When this happens, water rationing begins. Often this means you can't use the lawn sprinkler during the day or swimming pools can't be filled. There are things you can do to help your community get through the water shortage and drought.

Ways to Conserve Water

- Turn off the faucet while brushing your teeth
- Take shorter showers
- Only run the dishwasher or washing machine when full

THE DUST BOWL

The worst U.S. droughts in history happened during a series of heat waves in the 1930s. Between 1934 and 1936, farmers who were already strapped by the Great Depression saw their land turn dry and their crops die. The dust was so thick that 50 million acres in the Plains states (from Canada to Texas) became known as the Dust Bowl.

SANDSTORMS AND DUST STORMS

NOTHING TO SNEEZE AT

A dust storm descended over California's San Joaquin Valley on November 29, 1991. With visibility of 10 feet or less, Interstate 5 was the site of a traffic accident involving 164 cars, 151 injuries, and 17 deaths.

A SANDY STORM

To find a sandstorm you must have sand and lots of it, so expect them near deserts, beaches, dunes, and very, very large volleyball courts. The American Southwest, with its desert conditions, is a breeding ground for sandstorms. Across the globe, sandstorms are common in Saharan North Africa (where sandstorms are called siroccos), Mongolia's Gobi Desert, and India's Thar Desert.

Sandstorms are violent windstorms that come with a bonus: tons of sand in the air. The sand clouds can rise from 50 to 5,000 feet, while visibility (and traffic) drops down to almost nothing. The average sandstorm's wind speed is 10 mph, which is annoying but tolerable. But when the wind whips up to 40 or 50 mph, the rising and falling sand can feel like a swarm of stinging insects. Health problems from breathing sand are common.

The differences between a dust storm and a sandstorm seem small when you're in one, but are worth noting. Dust storms only occur in dry areas, usually during a drought. The particles are smaller in a dust storm too. Breathing is more difficult. And dust storms can kick up particles as high as 10,000 feet. The wind speed can reach over 30 mph and spread dust for hundreds of miles. The impact can shift sand dunes, erode precious soil, and bury roads—especially in the dry lands of the Western United States before the summer monsoon—and in the Great Plains states.

COLDEST PLACES

If you thrill to a big chill, then plan your next vacation in the coldest place on Earth: Antarctica. Clothes get stiff, eyelids freeze shut, teeth crack. It's where the world's lowest temperature was recorded: -128.6°F. So who lives there? A few human visitors, plus cold-adapted plants and animals. The emperor penguin, fur seals, mosses, and algae are all tough enough to survive the day-to-day average temperature of -57.5°F. OK, you say, but where's the coldest inhabited place? Welcome to Oimyakon in Russia's Siberia region. The 4,000 residents endure average temperatures of -60°F and occasional dips to -90°F. That's quite a bit colder than the average temperature on the Moon (-9°F) and not far off from Mars (-76°F).

CITY LIMITS Of America's five coldest cities, the first four are in Alaska and the first three begin with B (for brrrrr). Barrow and Barter Island, Alaska, each average 4°F. Bettles, Alaska, averages 12.9°F. Kotzebue, Alaska, surges to 15.3°F. And finally, Mount Washington, New Hampshire (home of the world's strongest wind) averages 19.8°F. Bring your earmuffs.

WIND CHILL When is cold even colder? When the wind is blowing. The wind chill factor is a measure of how cold the wind makes a person's skin feel. The wind can take 15°F or more off an already cold day. In 1975 the wind chill let locals in Canada's Northwest Territories know what -135°F feels like.

AN ICE PLACE TO LIVE

What are the cold, hard facts about the United States? The coldest recorded temperature was in McGrath, Alaska, when the mercury dipped to -75°F. Down in the lower 48 states, Williston, North Dakota, once dropped to -50°F.

FROZEN STATE

In February 1899, the United States saw its greatest cold wave: Every state registered below 0°F at the same time. (Hawaii wasn't a state then, and it's currently the only state that's never recorded a subzero temperature.) On average, the coldest states are Alaska, Minnesota, North Dakota, and Maine. Sled dogs are optional.

SNOWIE PLACES

WATERMELON SNOW

In California's Sierra Nevada mountains, watermelon snow is pink because it blends with an algae that is, of all things, green. Snow in other places across the globe has been black, blue, yellow, and red. In each event, something in the atmosphere (such as coal dust or pollen) was the added ingredient.

ST

If you don't live in snow country, you don't know the double joy of a snow day: School's cancelled, and you have the day free for snow business.

What makes the day off possible? In cold weather, wet heavy clouds lift and condense, and then out comes the snow. And get this: The same moisture in 1 inch of rain can equal 2 inches of slushy snow or as much as 40 inches of dry fluffy snow.

GREATEST SNOW ON EARTH The United States gets more than 100 snowstorms a year, and the high mountain ranges of the Western United States get more snow than anywhere else. The world's greatest single (measured) snowfall took place on California's Mount Shasta. From February 13 to 19 in 1959, 189 inches fell. That's almost 16 feet. Meanwhile, the world's heaviest seasonal snowfall was measured up north in Washington. That's where Mt. Baker Lodge recorded 1,140 inches (95 feet) in the winter of 1998–1999. It's no surprise: Locations with elevations higher than 2,000 feet almost always get more than 100 inches of snow each winter.

GET THE DRIFT The snowiest location in North America is on Mount Rainier in Washington, which receives an average of 680 inches per winter. Sometimes 30 feet of snow falls at a time. Rochester, New York is the snowiest city in the United States, averaging 94 inches of snow each year, and snowfalls in May are not uncommon. Every part of the United States except the Florida Keys has seen snow.

SNOW FOOLING

The colder it is outside, the smaller the snowflakes. An 8x12-inch snowflake—that's about the size of this page—was recorded in Bratsk, Siberia, in 1971. It must have been a warm day.

BLIZZARDS

Do you know what makes a snowstorm a blizzard? First the temperature goes down. Then the snow comes down—for at least three hours. Then the visibility is down to less than a quarter mile. (The winds are up, however, past 35 mph.) Next, of course, traffic slows to a standstill, and soon you're moving down the driveway with a shovel.

THE BIGGEST BLIZZARD The word blizzard once meant a rapid attack from cannon or rifle fire. Then back in '88—that's 1888—came America's record-setting blizzard. From March 11 to 13, the northeastern United States suffered near-hurricane winds, temperatures near zero, and more than 50 inches of snow. Houses, trains, and people were buried. More than 400 people perished and more than 200 ships were damaged or lost. The collapsed phone and power lines in New York City spurred a new city law requiring all cables to be run underground.

WHITEOUT A whiteout is a blizzard that's so overwhelming that visibility is nearly impossible. Downdrafts of air mix with snow to create a white wall, which can get anyone confused and lost.

SNOW MOVER

The world's largest snowplow works at the Syracuse, New York airport with a blade that's 32 feet wide and 4 feet high. It can clear 8,500 cubic yards of snow each hour, which is equlivalent to 3.42 million half-gallons of ice cream.

WE'RE OFF TO SEE THE BLIZZARD

Between 1960 and 2000, more blizzards struck western Minnesota, North Dakota, and South Dakota than any other states. Take heart: The United States only averages 11 blizzards a year.

ICE STORMS

What can make you truly wish for a good, strong blizzard? An ice storm. The clouds darken, the frozen stuff comes out of the sky, and the damage begins. The ice gets heavier and heavier as it accumulates, sometimes many inches thick. Frozen tree branches crack off. Ice-laden trees topple. Power lines go down just when you need electricity the most. Roads are treacherous. Garage doors won't open, and if they do, cars get stuck to their driveways. Only the very worst snowstorms can do more damage.

But when the storm stops and the sun comes out, the world is a crystal wonderland. Everything—every twig on the remaining trees—is glazed in glistening, gorgeous ice. Ice storms are different than mere freezing rain and less frequent. Ice storms occur when warm, humid air collides with frigid Arctic air, generally in the northeastern United States. The falling near-ice freezes on contact; each new layer gets colder, thicker, and more dangerous.

BLACK ICE

Black ice isn't black, but it is deadly. This transparent form of ice blends in with highway asphalt, making it appear black and creating slick and hazardous conditions for unaware drivers.

ICE CUBED The biggest ice storms occur only every few years and can strike anywhere between Texas and upper Canada. The thickest, slickest accumulation of ice from a single storm—8 inches—fell on northern Idaho on January 1–3, 1961. The 1998 ice storm that shut down New England was especially destructive, causing more than $600 million in damage.

SLEET

Sleet is made up of really small, partially melted ice pellets with a twist: Sleet bounces when it lands. But where does it come from? Sleet begins as raindrops, which then fall through different air layer temperatures. If any layer is below the freezing point, the raindrops become sleet. Snowflakes can become sleet if they melt before they freeze. Wear a hat. Use an umbrella. Sleet hurts.

RAINIEST PLACES

Rain, rain go away? Not likely in these water-filled wonderlands. Special combinations of temperature, topography (mountains and such), nearby water, and other factors decide who gets a little rain and who gets drenched.

WORLD'S WETTEST The United States has many accomplishments, and this one is all wet. Hawaii's Kauai Island averages 470 inches of precipitation each year—which is about 39 feet! And with an average temperature of 75°F, you can bet none of it is snow. And speaking of Hawaii, 108 inches of rain (9 feet!) fell at Pu'u Kukui, in Maui in March 1942. It was the wettest month ever in the United States. You can bet that's not on the travel brochure.

FOG FACTS

Don't be in a fog about fog. It's just a low-flying cloud and a great start to any mystery story. When the temperature drops below dewpoint and the relative humidity reaches 100 percent, the water vapor condenses. Hello, fog. And it can say goodbye quickly too; when the day gets warmer, the fog burns off.

NEWS DROP

Raindrops are not shaped like teardrops. They are nearly spherical and are 2 millimeters in diameter. Larger raindrops (2 to 6 millimeters) are similar in shape to a hamburger bun.

RAIN FORESTS

Any forest that receives more than 8 feet of rain each year qualifies as a rain forest. Amazingly, the Amazon, the world's largest tropical rain forest, and other rain forests hold over half of all plant and animal species on Earth—but cover less than 8 percent of the planet. The only tropical rain forest in the United States is El Yunque in eastern Puerto Rico—a territory of the United States with commonwealth status. In its higher elevations, El Yunque gets more than 20 feet of rain each year.

THUNDERSTORMS

When it comes to thunderstorms, the United States takes the world by storm. Nowhere (except possibly India and Bangladesh) will you find the slamming, slashing, crashing sky shows that are made in America. Why the United States? Because it sits between dependable sources of warm, moist, unstable air (the Gulf of Mexico) and cool, dry, stable air (the Arctic north). Any time the two fronts meet, there can be a real collision.

FIRST COMES LIGHTNING Lightning is what electricity looks like. It's a form of static discharge, not much different than the little electrical shock created when you shuffle your feet and touch a metal doorknob—except lightning contains a billion volts of electricity. That kind of voltage will light a 25-watt bulb for a year, though lightning actually looks more like 100 million lightbulbs going on and off.

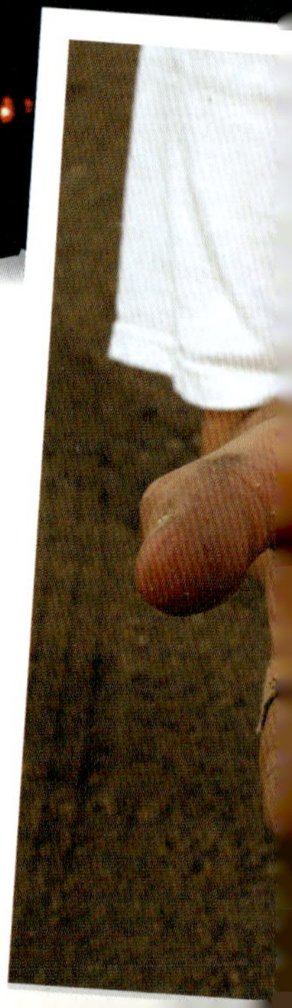

THEN COMES THUNDER Not only is lightning bright, it's hot. (Some say more than 50,000°F—that's about six times hotter than the surface of the sun.) That kind of heat makes the gases in the air heat up quickly and expand. Guess what happens to things that heat up and expand? They make a noise. A loud noise. How loud depends mostly on how close the lightning strikes to the listener. Every 5 seconds between lightning and thunder equals a mile of distance. So if you count 10 seconds, the lightning strike is 2 miles away. And so on.

HOW BIG?

A bolt of lightning is only about half an inch thick. It just looks bigger due to the luminosity.

ALL HAIL

Besides rain, thunderstorm clouds also drop hail, which are little balls of ice. Hail is usually the size of a pea but can be as large as a softball. Just because hail is ice, don't think this phenomenon occurs in the winter. Hail is common during strong thunderstorms that occur in the spring and summer.

Of all the weather-related natural disasters, floods are the most common. This is due in part to the fact that floods can strike anywhere, anytime, any day of the year. Flooding usually, but not always, follows a devastating rain. Flooding can also occur after winter snow melts, dam or levee breaks, or when the ground is just too wet and it can't absorb any more water. Floodwater can range anywhere from a few inches of water to enough to cover a house.

There are basically two types of floods. The first, river floods, is when the water in a river slowly rises—due to snow melting or heavy seasonal rain. Eventually the water spills over its banks, usually for miles around. The second type, flash floods, is more dangerous as they can happen very quickly, without warning. Flash floods can occur within several seconds of a heavy rain or up to six hours afterward when the water levels in a small stream, gulley, or river basin rise quickly, with a forceful current. Flash flood waters are so strong they can destroy buildings, wash away bridges, and erode the earth that holds up structures.

MAJOR U.S. FLOODS The Great Flood of 1889 was also known as the Johnstown Flood. Extremely heavy rain caused the South Fork Dam to fail near Johnstown, Pennsylvania. Some 20 million gallons of water (equivalent to 30 Olympic-size swimming pools) flooded the town.

America's deadliest regional flood: the Ohio River Flood of 1913. Four days of unending rain caused water to rise 18 feet (up to the third floor of some buildings) before the waters receded. When the Mississippi and Missouri rivers flooded in 1993, more than 22,000 homes (and some towns) were destroyed.

BIG FLOODS

BE CAREFUL

Flood Watch
flooding is possible due to the current weather conditions.

Flood Warning
flooding may be happening in your area; take necessary precautions.

100-YEAR FLOOD Q&A

QUESTION: If a 100-year flood occurs when you're in the eighth grade, can it occur again before you reach the age of 87?

ANSWER: Yes, because the term, 100-year flood, actually refers to the chance of a 100-year flood occurring in any year, which is 1 percent. The term is confusing, because you'd think it meant that a 100-year flood could only happen once every 100 years. However, every flood season has the same chance of producing a 100-year flood, just like every time you flip a coin, there is a chance it will come up tails.

TSUNAMIS

Tsunamis—powerful and destructive waves—are generated under the sea when there's an earthquake, landslide, or volcanic eruption. The water shakes and the giant waves follow. Before breaking on shore, the waves can tower 100 feet high (or higher) and be more than 50 miles long. The ocean water can rush forward at 450 mph or faster, which is the same speed as an airplane. Tsunamis do the most damage when they strike near the shore and can inundate areas that are normally up to 30 feet above sea level.

Tsunamis are giant killers, and many victims usually drown in the rushing walls of water. Because the waves can come 30 to 60 minutes apart, many who die are those who rush to the beach after the first wave strikes, believing there won't be any more. But there will be more, because a tsunami is actually a series of waves, rippling out in circles from an epicenter. If you see one coming when you're on the beach, you need to be on higher ground to survive.

THE INDIAN OCEAN TSUNAMI

The deadliest tsunami in history was on December 26, 2004. The waves traveled up to 5,000 miles across the open ocean without losing much of their power. About 230,000 people from eastern Africa, India, Thailand, and other countries were killed—most of the victims (168,000) from Indonesia.

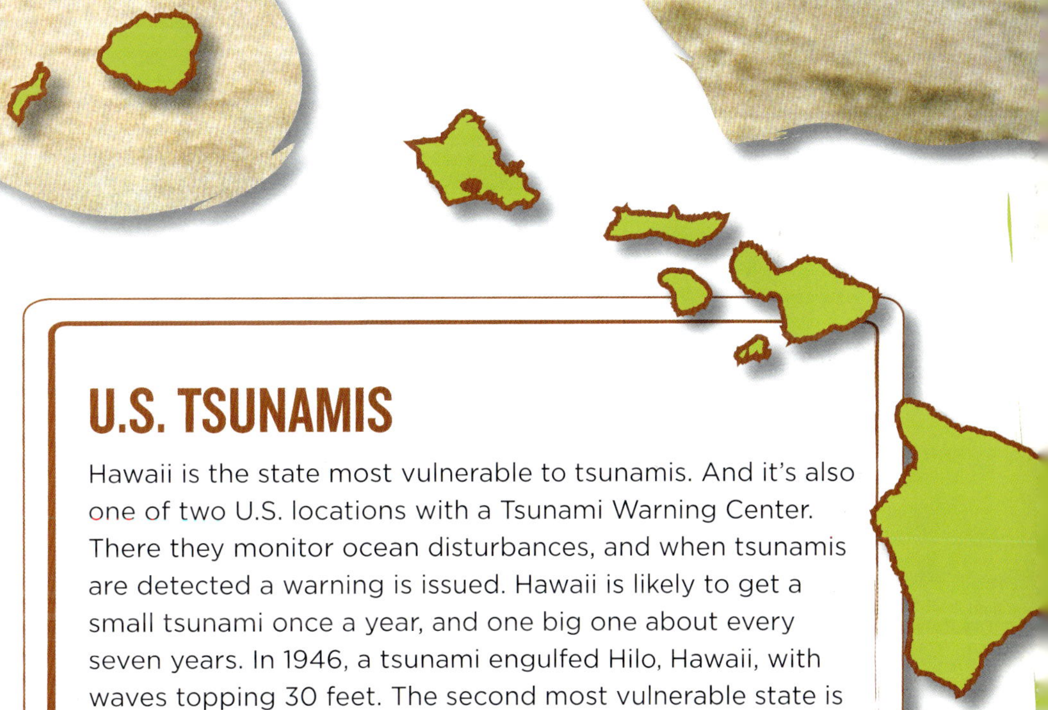

U.S. TSUNAMIS

Hawaii is the state most vulnerable to tsunamis. And it's also one of two U.S. locations with a Tsunami Warning Center. There they monitor ocean disturbances, and when tsunamis are detected a warning is issued. Hawaii is likely to get a small tsunami once a year, and one big one about every seven years. In 1946, a tsunami engulfed Hilo, Hawaii, with waves topping 30 feet. The second most vulnerable state is Alaska, which also has a Tsunami Warning Center. The other Pacific Coast states—Washington, Oregon, and California—were hit in 1964 by waves reaching 20 feet high.

What makes the earth quake? The planet's outer crust is covered with giant plates, like panels of a soccer ball. Those plates are always shifting in slow, slow motion, and occasionally something drops. The resulting vibrations (which can flatten a city) are called earthquakes. Quakes happen along the fault lines between plates. For the record, volcanoes, meteors, and explosions also can cause earthquakes, but these events are much less frequent.

CALIFORNIA ROCKS California is well-known for its movies, its oranges, its weather, and about 10,000 earthquakes a year. Most can be ignored because they're too small to feel. However, the great San Francisco earthquake of April 18, 1906 (8.25 magnitude) could not be. It lasted about 40 seconds, and one survivor compared it to riding down the stairs on a bicycle. The extensive damage to the city wasn't actually caused by the quake but by the fires—fueled by broken natural gas mains, arsonists, and refugees living in makeshift campsites—that raged for days after. Approximately 2,500 people died. The 1989 Loma Prieta earthquake (7.1 magnitude) in the San Francisco area became known as the World Series earthquake because it struck just as a World Series championship baseball game was being played at the local stadium. Los Angeles' 1994 Northridge earthquake was magnitude 6.7.

BIG BANGS The world's largest recorded earthquake stirred Chile on May 22, 1960. It was a magnitude 9.5 quake, which caused great damage. Fortunately, America's largest recorded earthquake happened in a desolate place: A magnitude 9.2 quake struck Alaska's Prince William Sound on March 28, 1964. Want to play it safe? Florida and North Dakota have had the fewest earthquakes. Want to live life on the edge (of a fault line)? Alaska is America's shakiest state, getting a 7.0 quake every year or so, and an 8.0 earthquake about every 14 years.

EARTHQ

MR. RICHTER'S SCALE

Developed by Charles Richter in 1935, the Richter Scale is our method for measuring an earthquake's intensity, or magnitude.

4.0	Little or no damage
5.0	Shakes and some damage
6.0	Strong, with much damage
7.0	Major earthquake, major damage
8.0+	If you live, you'll have quite a story

Each increase of 1 represents a 32-fold increase in released energy.

IN CASE OF QUAKE

Drop onto the floor, get under something solid (a strong table or a solid doorway), and hold on until the shaking stops. Earthquakes are almost always less than a minute long.

UAKES

The world has at least 500 active volcanoes. Many of them circle the Pacific Ocean in an area called the Ring of Fire. But the country with the most volcanoes is Indonesia.

The United States has its fair share of active volcanoes too. Hawaii and Alaska, with more than 100 volcanoes, have the most people at risk. But the residents in Washington, Oregon, and California know all about volcanic eruptions too. The lower 48 states have about 40 active volcanoes.

What's a volcano, really? It's a mountain with an opening that leads to molten rock below the Earth's surface. Every now and then, pressure builds and out comes lava, gas, and rocks into the air. Some rocks fly out at 300 mph. Volcanoes can cause earthquakes, floods, tsunamis, and avalanches. And you thought it was just the lava you had to worry about.

LETHAL LAVA Volcanic lava burns; volcanic rocks crush cars; volcanic ash can damage lungs. In 1815, Mount Tambora erupted in Indonesia, killing 92,000 people, blocking the sun with volcanic ash and causing summer snowfalls as far away as North America. When Mount Krakatoa blew its top, Indonesia saw 36,000 people die in 1883. On May 18, 1980, in Washington, the volcano called Mount Saint Helen's erupted after having been dormant for 100 years, killing 58 people and causing more than $1.2 billion in damage. In the Philippine Islands, Mount Pinatubo (which was not suspected of being volcanic) erupted in 1992, killing 342 people and displacing more than 250,000.

VOLCANO

VOLCANO BELIEVE IT?

More than 80 percent of the Earth's surface was created by volcanoes, including many mountains and the ocean floor. The world's biggest volcano is Hawaii's Mauna Loa, which rises 29,000 feet from the ocean floor (including 13,000 feet above sea level). The world's oldest volcano is Sicily's Mount Etna, which is about 350,000 years old. It is also a volcanic giant. And Crater Lake in Oregon was formed when a volcano blew its top about 6,700 years ago.

WINDIEST PLACES

Which natural disaster can be heard and felt but not seen? And what's the windiest city in the United States? The answer is blowing in the wind.

GET OUT OF DODGE The National Climatic Data Center says the windiest U.S. city is Dodge City, Kansas, with average winds of 14 mph. The city was probably named by people who were dodging flying buildings, cattle, and so on. The next windiest cities are Amarillo, Texas (averaging 13.5 mph winds) and Rochester, Minnesota (averaging wind speeds of 13.1 mph). Hold on to your hat!

WINDS UP California hosts two predictable, powerful winds that sometimes cause deep devastation. Southern California has the Santa Ana winds, and the Diablo winds blow through the San Francisco area. Both winds bring hot, dry air that carries and feeds wildfires. In 1991, a fire in the Oakland Hills near San Francisco raged for days, burning more than 3,500 homes and killing 25 people. In 2003, the Santa Ana winds took 3,500 homes (and 20 lives) in a wildfire that torched more than 1,000 square miles.

MEASURING UP

Wind speed is calculated with an anemometer, a cupped propeller that spins in the wind. Wind speed is measured in knots, each of which is equal to 1.15 mph. Wind force is measured on the Beaufort Wind Scale.

Beaufort Wind Scale

Force	Wind Speed	Classification	Appearance on Land
1	less than 1 Knot	Calm	Smoke rises vertically
4	11–16 Knots	Moderate Breeze	Small tree branches move
6	22–27 Knots	Strong Breeze	Larger tree branches move
8	34–40 Knots	Gale	Whole trees in motion
10	48–55 Knots	Storm	Trees broken or uprooted
11	56–63 Knots	Violent Storm	*30- to 45-foot waves
12	64+ Knots	Hurricane	*Waves over 45 feet

* does not happen on land

AMERICA'S WINDIEST

The wildest wind in the country is recorded regularly at New Hampshire's Mount Washington Observatory, where the average wind speed is 35 mph. On April 12, 1934, a world's record surface wind of 231 mph was recorded there. Number two is Massachusetts's Blue Hill Observatory, averaging more than 15 miles per hour.

HURRICANES, CYCLONES, AND TYPHOONS

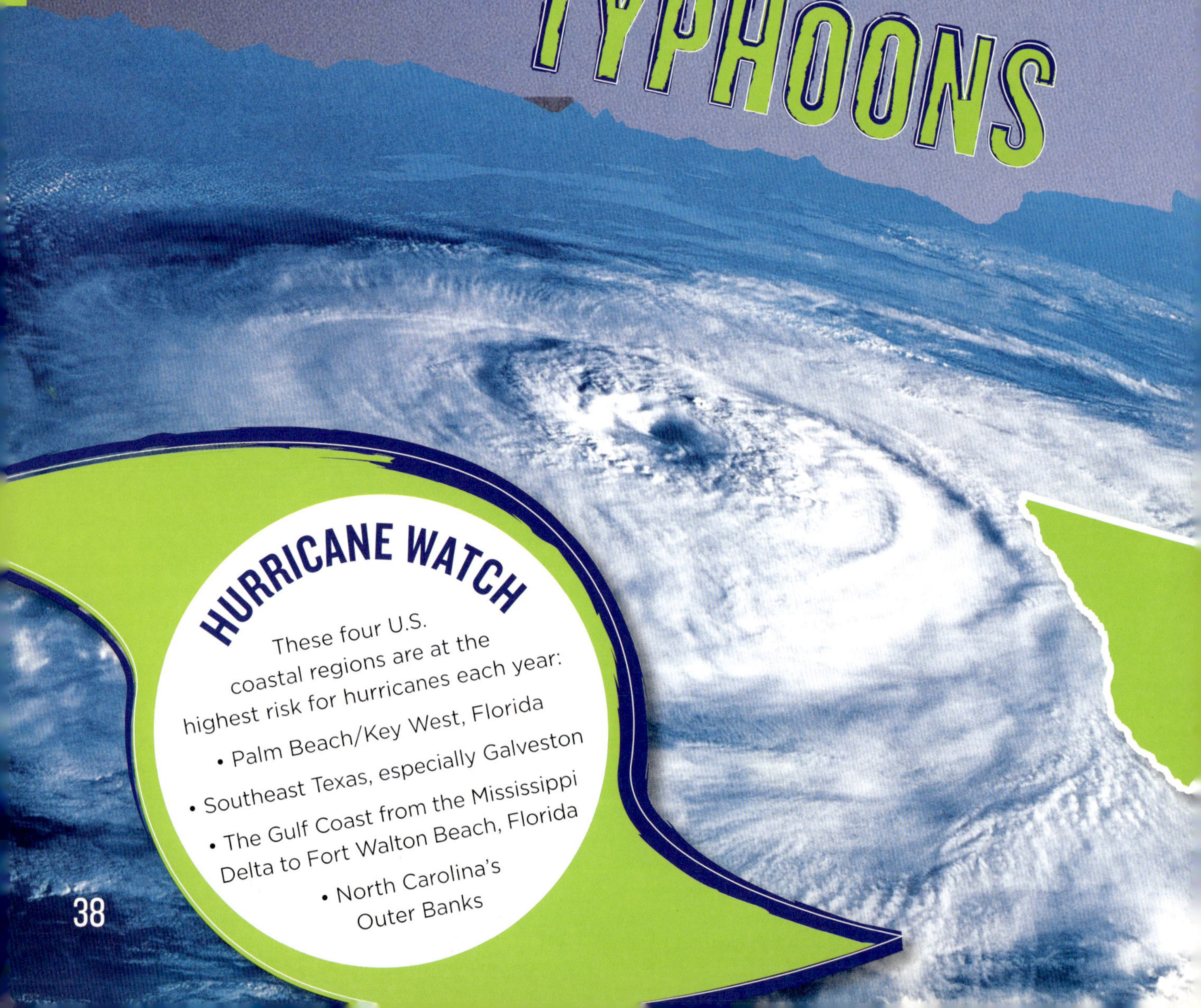

HURRICANE WATCH

These four U.S. coastal regions are at the highest risk for hurricanes each year:

- Palm Beach/Key West, Florida
- Southeast Texas, especially Galveston
- The Gulf Coast from the Mississippi Delta to Fort Walton Beach, Florida
- North Carolina's Outer Banks

What's the difference between a hurricane, a cyclone, and a typhoon? The spelling and location, and not much else. Each is a severe tropical storm, built the same way and able to do lots of damage. From the mid-1800s to Hurricane Katrina in 2005, hurricanes have killed more than 21,000 Americans. And that's a conservative estimate.

Deadlier than a tornado, a hurricane is a spiraling, low-pressure air mass that builds over the ocean. Once that mass is surrounded by warm, humid air, the ingredients for storm damage are in place. High winds carry a wall of water, called a storm surge, to the shore. Coastal areas are flooded and often destroyed by the wind, flooding, and whatever's been flying through the air. Shutter and board your windows and wait it out.

HURRICANE KATRINA

The devastating Hurricane Katrina wasn't America's most deadly hurricane, but it was the most damaging. It was also the second Category 5 (winds greater than 155 mph) hurricane in the United States in 2005. Katrina brought the highest costs of any hurricane too. The damage to the Gulf Coast (especially to New Orleans, where levees broke and neighborhoods were flooded) was severe and will take decades to repair.

AMERICA'S DEADLIEST

The Galveston Hurricane of September 8, 1900, in Texas ranks as the country's worst. Winds exceeded 120 mph. Water rose at 1 foot per second. About 10,000 people died, as did many more sailors at sea. Every home in Galveston was damaged.

TORNADOES

Welcome to the United States: tornado capital of the world. On average anywhere from 800 to 1,000 tornadoes each year give the United States a spin. That's about half of all the tornadoes reported on Earth.

Tornadoes have the circular suction power to topple fully grown trees—roots and all. A considerable or severe tornado, whirling between 100 and 200 mph, tears off roofs and flips over cars. The strongest tornadoes have been clocked with winds near 250 mph, which can send a house flying and then smashing down against its own driveway. Survivors say when a tornado arrives, it sounds like a swarm of bees, heavy lightning, or a freight train.

Not all tornadoes look like funnels. Some appear to be solid sheets of wind and rain. Either way, as the twister starts twisting, it picks up rocks, mailboxes, and everything that it can carry, which is a lot. Within a few seconds up to hours, the tornado runs out of steam, and it ends up like a wet, wrung-out vertical towel before it stops altogether. But you're not safe yet: Remember all that heavy stuff kicking around and around? There's no more force holding it up in the air—and down it comes!

WORLD'S DEADLIEST TORNADO

One twister in Bangladesh killed more than 1,300 people on April 25, 1989.

WILD WEATHER

Every state in the union has reported at least one tornado. But there's no place like Oklahoma; no other state gets more tornadoes.

NIGHT FLIGHT

On March 12, 2006, 19-year-old Matt Suter of Missouri earned a world record as the luckiest person to survive being carried by a tornado. He flew 1,307 feet. The previous record holders, a girl and her pony, from South Dakota had been tossed 1,000 feet in 1955 and were not hurt.

WATERSP

AND

WATER WITH A TWIST

One sailing ship, the Lilian Morris, was ripped up by a 500-foot-wide waterspout that flung a man overboard. A waterspout off the coastal African nation of Tunis sunk five ships. And closer to home, a waterspout once flipped over a shrimping boat and sank it in San Antonio Bay in Texas.

OUTS

MICROBURSTS

Waterspouts are tornadoes that develop over water. They're common in south Florida (especially in the Florida Keys) from May to September. Waterspouts are long, thin, and dangerous. The funnels literally suck water out of the ocean (or lake or river) and spray it through the top like a whale or a fountain. But there are some key differences. Waterspouts are more common than tornadoes. They're also weaker and rarely do the damage of a powerful tornado. But they're a force to be reckoned with, especially when they sometimes reach land.

Some waterspouts are only a few feet high and a few feet wide. Others get going to a mile high and several hundred feet wide. Sailors especially fear waterspouts on the open water because waterspouts are like vacuums and suck up anything in their path. Here's what happens: First, sailors hear a great hissing or sucking sound. Then come the gale-force winds, up to 80 mph. Anything that ends up inside the waterspout is thrashed around in winds that can blow more than 120 mph. This can last up to 15 minutes, with a few lasting more than a half hour.

MICROBURSTS These thunderless thunderstorms are small, powerful downbursts of wind less than 2.5 miles in diameter. As the downburst, which is a strong downdraft, leaves a cloud base it begins to pick up speed and within minutes it strikes the ground. The highest winds (170 mph or more) are recorded when it strikes the ground. The effects of microbursts are similar to a non-moving tornado.

FLYING FISH

Sometimes an umbrella just isn't enough. Waterspouts can rain amazing things on not-so-lucky people. Tadpoles were sprayed in New York. Lizards showered Montreal, Canada, and fish fell on Providence, Rhode Island, which were promptly collected and sold at market.

MONSOO

The word monsoon means shifting wind, and a monsoon climate isn't all wet: It's any climate that shifts back and forth seasonally between wetter and drier seasons. Monsoons bring severe rainy seasons that can overwhelm a region with nonstop downpours. In India, which is famous for its monsoons, hundreds of inches of rain can fall in one place in one year. But it's not all floods and fear. Many people living in monsoon regions depend on these seasonal downpours for the water they use during the dry season.

India's wet southwest monsoons occur in the warmer months, from about May to October, when the dry winds reverse direction and blow in from over the Indian Ocean. That's where all the moisture comes from. The drier winds are called the retreating monsoon, but they don't retreat for long.

MADE IN AMERICA The American Southwest has a monsoon of its own, coincidentally also called the southwest monsoon. Once August rolls in, so do the clouds; massive thunderstorms overtake the region, bringing water to parched Western lands after all the dry months. These powerful rainstorms are fed by humid air from the Gulf of Mexico and the Gulf of California.

NS

RAIN? MAN!

Cherrapunji, India, holds two world records for precipitation—thanks to its monsoons. In July 1861, this Himalayan community was hit with the most rain in a single month: 366 inches, which is more than 12 inches a day. The other record? That month capped the wettest year ever recorded. From August 1860 to July 1861, 1,042 inches of rain fell.

GLOBAL WARMING

In the Northern Hemisphere, the spring thaw generally comes 9 days earlier than it did in 1850. The autumn freeze comes 10 days later. Average temperatures on Earth have risen 1°F in the past 100 years and may rise between 2°F and 6°F in the next 100. What's causing the Earth to heat up?

Scientists agree that this climate change has primarily been caused by human activity. Why blame humans? Because no other animal burns fossil fuels, cuts down forests, or paves the planet with heat-absorbing tar. As the impact of humans grows, more carbon dioxide enters the atmosphere, which is retaining more heat. This is known as the greenhouse effect.

WHAT TO EXPECT Climate change affects every living thing on Earth. More rain falls, ice caps and glaciers melt, and the sea level rises. Coastal regions and low-lying islands are beginning to flood and disappear under water. Ecosystems and habitats are being threatened. Food and water supplies are being affected. People in hotter areas—especially the young and the elderly—will be at risk of sickness or death from the heat. Whole species of animals and plants that cannot adapt may perish. What can you do to turn this around?

WHAT TO DO

The good news is that the effects of global warming are reversible. The urgent news is that humans need to reduce their impact on the planet immediately. Burning less fuel in cars and homes, recycling more, and using renewable energy sources like solar power and wind power are all excellent first steps. For more information, log on to www.Discovery.com and search for "Global Warming."

Remember, humans made this mess, and we're the only ones who can begin cleaning it up.

GLOSSARY

Aftershock: a minor shock following a large earthquake in the same region

Altitude: the height of an object above land or sea level

Anemometer: a device that measures and records the force or speed of the wind

Arid: an extremely dry climate

Atmosphere: the layer of gases surrounding the planet Earth

Cold wave: a sudden drop in temperature within a 24-hour period

Dam: a barrier built across water to control the flow or raise the water level

Dew point: the temperature at which air becomes saturated and produces dew

Downdraft: a sudden descent of cool or cold air to the ground

Dust bowl: a region that suffers from long droughts and dust storms

Earth's crust: the outer part of the Earth

Elevation: the height of something above land or sea level

Erosion: the process by which the Earth's surface is worn away by wind or water

Freezing rain: rain that falls as liquid and freezes upon impact to form a coating of ice on the ground or other exposed surfaces

Great Plains: natural grassland that stretches eastward of the Rocky Mountains from Canada to New Mexico and includes all or part of Montana, Wyoming, North Dakota, South Dakota, Nebraska, Colorado, Kansas, Oklahoma, Texas, and New Mexico

Groundwater: water beneath the Earth's surface, often between saturated soil and rock that supplies wells and springs

Heat wave: a period of unusually hot weather lasting from several days to several weeks

Hot ash flow: extremely hot volcanic ash and debris that roll quickly down the sides of a volcano

La Niña: unusually cold ocean temperatures in the tropical Pacific Ocean area

Lava: molten rock that can be erupted from a volcano

Levee: an embankment that's designed to prevent a river from overflowing

Mud slides: a landslide of mud

Natural disaster: any catastrophic force of nature not caused by human activity: avalanche, earthquake, flood, hurricane, lightning, tornado, tsunami, and volcanic eruption

Palmer Index: uses temperature and rainfall information in a formula to determine dryness, often associated with drought

Precipitation: any form of water that falls to the Earth's surface: drizzle, rain, hail, ice crystals, sleet, and snow

Richter Scale: measures earthquake intensity on a scale of 1 to 10

Saffir-Simpson Scale: measures hurricane intensity on a scale of 1 to 5

Sediment: solid inorganic or organic fragments that come from the weathering of rock, and are carried and deposited by wind, water, or ice

Snowpack: the amount of annual accumulation of snow at higher elevations

Tidal wave: a huge destructive wave that sometimes follows an earthquake